Commute

A Poetry Collection

Other Books By Oskar Leonard:

Intricacies Inked In Ice
Our Paused World
Aleatory Poetry

Commute

A Poetry Collection

By Oskar Leonard

For George - thank you for being there for me through everything.

Contents Page

Introduction

Commute is a collection of poems relating to travel. Specifically the many journeys Oskar Leonard has taken in recent years as well as the personal journeys of thought he has had while undertaking them. There are countless glimpses into the writer's experiences, thoughts, and imagination loosely concealed in this book and I count myself lucky to have been privy to as many of the referred to events I was. It is fascinating reading about the ones I wasn't too. Oskar is allowing us a glimpse through his eyes via his writing here and it is tremendously intriguing to see his perception of the world, how it differs from my own as well as the similarities.

You can see the end and beginning of different things in this collection, told in a non-chronological order that makes every consecutive poem a piece of writing that you can turn to and fall into fresh. You can flick to a random page and find yourself a little uncertain, a little curious, and waiting 'til you reach the end to properly digest it. Just like anyone riding a new bus route, taking a train they haven't before, or treading down an unfamiliar track. Every commute shared with us is a commute that we can now be a part of. That we can watch. All from the perspective of the little record keeper that sits in the back of Oskar's mind, committing the feelings and worries to memory only to be recalled here for us.

Truth be told, I think I would be too scared to create such a collection of poems that reflect on the workings of my mind and publish them to the world. It seems Oskar is a braver man than I, and I can respect that. I've been able to watch and listen as these poems were written, and let me tell you as someone who is constantly gifted notebooks that I know I'll never write in, it is awe-inspiring watching this man go through maybe six or eight poems in a single sitting and cross them off his list. Watching him put pen to paper and leave his words scrawled across the page with reckless abandon, only to redraft and edit them later when he types them up... not only the ability to commit so easily, but the fact that he went through the events these poems referred to once, summed up the courage to write them down, and then properly revisit them for redrafting to share them with us? I know I'm impressed, and given how well written and engaging the poems and the memories they allude to are, both you and he should be too.

It was nearly a year ago that I met Oskar Leonard, and to tell the truth, I cannot properly emphasise how he shot up in my estimation. He went from being a slightly nervous first year in need of some hospitality, to a peer worthy of my respect, to someone who was leaps and bounds ahead of me in a field I took pride in. Oskar became someone for me to emulate and learn from, someone whose existence in my social sphere pushed me to better myself and my writing and I will forever appreciate that. Given this particular collection's themes I thought it was worth ending my introduction with an explanation of the journey he has undertaken in my mind since we met.

It is an honour for me to write an introduction to one of his books, and I hope you enjoy reading Commute as I did.

-George Knott.

Section I - By Bus

Commute Horror Show (320)

5.30 AM--the bus driver has blood
on his fingertips, clutching the wheel
with an early morning death grip.

Towards the stairs--she's wearing the skins
of her last three pet cats, still pulsing
with their final panicked breaths.

Top deck--two skeletons chatter
while puffing smoke out of mimic lungs,
staring each other down with borrowed eyes.

Backseat--between the engine's growls,
faint screams echo through the metal:
poor souls who stayed on past the last stop.

Rescue (38)

Never accept rides from strangers,
unless they're your saviours from Rainford--
with a missing 152 on a cold afternoon,
one elderly face, name unknown,
rolls down a window at the side of the road.

'Would you like a lift?' And the alarm bells
ring just like the stop button would,
yet now that village is your destination
and you're perched on a stranger's backseat
quivering at primary school memories.

Stranger danger, yes, but your fingers
were turning to an ashen white--
and you're older now, and that face
was one you knew, vaguely, from the bus stop
for the 152--oh, it'll be alright.

Your saviours drop you off by a bus stop,
as a bus disappears around the corner.
You thank them all the same, never give them
your name, and embrace a thirty-minute wait
for that same turquoise bus, coming round again.

Long-Suffering (152)

Oh, poor thing. Poor us, passengers,
sitting--or standing--
and wondering whether our bus--
our little green 152, our once-every-two-hours,
only route to Ormskirk bus,
would show up at all.

Oh, lovely thing. Lovely us, passengers,
finally gathered in our seats,
shepherded by an amiable driver--
onto our sun-soaked 152, humming through Crank,
all on our way to Ormskirk;
past rolling fields, yawning horses.

Oh, inconsistent thing. Inconsistent us, passengers,
because only some faces remain
the same, day-on-day--
we, the 152 regulars, the 7.15 and 4.24,
to and from our Ormskirk regulars,
when our bus shows up,

and does not abandon us.

Roundabout (EL1)

How do you keep your smile
when all you do is go around
and around, and then around
again, from the crack of dawn
to the end of the day?

Perhaps it is leisurely;
no more than a dream,
with your fingertips drifting
from steering wheel to indicator,
then back again.

But no, not me--I couldn't imagine
the monotony--the same roads,
trees, faces, over and over,
day on day; surely, months
must turn all into a muddy blur.

Elephant In The Room (395)

Silhouette in pink, waiting
under the shade of a vape shop
to travel to a graffitied park
and sit on a bird shit covered bench,
talking about everything except
what we should discuss--what we both
feel we have an obligation to speak of,
yet neither of us wish to disturb the screams
of toddlers with our sense and emotion,
so the silhouette returns, waving off a bus,
and the elephant remains.

Taking You Home With Me (375)

Night. I know, logically, you shouldn't
be here. You should have seen me off
at the bus station--we should have
already said our goodbyes, shed our tears.

Yet we didn't. Our night goes on,
and you remain at my side,
snuggled into me and promising
that you will stay, no matter what life dictates.

Night. Our fingers reach for the button
and skin blushes, knuckles giggle into each other
as we do leave, both of us, but this time--
just for tonight--we leave together, side by side.

We All Make Mistakes (10A)

You think you can get away
with your wrong turn--but no.

We are here. We, your arch enemies;
we, the teenagers.

This is our bus--our morningly
and nightly commute.

And you have taken the wrong turn,
haven't you?

Our voices rise, and you must (non-verbally)
admit to your mistake.

We will wait. We witness your pain-staking
reversal, and we know that you now know

that this is our bus, and we, benevolent
as we are known to be, forgive you

through giggles.

To Break, To Repair (34)

It was never meant to be
like this--but neither of us
could've known, or seen,
this future--this journey.

Together now, but at another
point we will drift apart--glass
always shatters when you put it
under enough pressure,

and the weight of this--
of us--of you... I'm sorry,
but I'm not, because it's
the essence of self-preservation.

There would be no me
left to repair, if there
continued to be a broken
us, a shuddering us.

Long Way Home (310)

Can you drift aimlessly through clouds
on a haze of Poison and Motley
like I can? As evening becomes dark,
and I know that I could've just--could've
simply taken the quick route home,
the shortcut, expensive but fast--
yet there is no magic in ease,
or an empty bank account;
beauty is blood on a bus ticket.

The Darkest Hour (10)

Two nurses discuss their daily woes:
fights, struggles, lunches and foes,
as even teenagers keep their music low
and the engine grumbles idly below.

With every departure, another gasp
of silence fills the deadening lapse,
and time crumbles out of my grasp
with another encore of the driver's rasp.

We'll all be home by the end of the night,
some of us enduring a flashing blue fright
while others collapse and turn off the light
after clinging to consciousness with all our might.

Confused (9)

My obligations have grown
seven obligations of their own,
until my responsibilities tremble
in the shadow of their dependants
and I wonder how one mind
can be expected to keep it all together.

Is it any wonder that the nerves,
so put-upon, crack? Wrong bus,
wrong way; but who cares?
Not me. Life has sucked, completely
sucked, all the caring
right out of me.

How Are You Different? (385)

In the case of twins,
how do you tell the two
apart?

You cannot simply dissect them,
pulling away the metal to reveal the
heart.

And the bother of comparing
routes on paper, well--I
can't.

I suppose the only way
is to ensure to mark them at the
start.

A '7' and an '8' will
surely be able to play a
part.

A Change Of Scenery (156)

Yes, you can consider
life to be much easier
with shorter journeys,
which allow you to fall
into your bed far quicker.

But then--oh, then
you would miss out
on the life--on the
faces, the trees,
every little dog

with a wagging tail,
bright eyes--you
would've never seen it
on your direct route--
take a minute, breathe.

Split-Second (Coach)

I decided in a second--
yes, one of madness,
drenched in hope
and cliche--
to change my life forever,
and I'm so glad I did.

One step on--one step
down the aisle, then
another, between the
seats, and my fate,
otherwise fluctuating,
became concrete.

It saw you, smiled,
and took my hand.

I Miss You (559)

I mark the days on my calendar,
and in my diary, just for good measure.

They turn into weeks which bleed,
hauntingly, into months, and I cry.

In a better world, my pillow would become
your soft chest--but we don't live there.

Distances are only numbers and times
are only numbers, but love isn't numbers.

Isn't. Wasn't. Love becomes '559'--love becomes
the vessel on which you ride towards me.

It will take you away, as well; I know this,
and I cry, but they are happy tears:

I will see you again.

Company (2)

Lowest hours demand
the least company--
yet you must resist,
and surround yourself
with the warmest faces
to exist, who will drag you
to places, and on buses,
and laugh with you
or scream with you,
because they care,
and no one needs to do
anything more
than simply care.

Irony (666)

Don't talk to me
of irony
until you've bypassed
the 665
to take a sinful route
to your catholic college.

Sure, they both
go the same way--
yes, they both
end up in the same place
(otherwise, what use
is a college bus?).

Yet riding on
the 666--
it tastes of crime,
and stinks of curses
and the Devil's armpit,
and we are teenagers.

Do Not Move Us (657)

One route may be swelling
until the bus is fit to bursting,
ripe with the stench of deodorant
and burning plastic,
but that doesn't mean that we will leave
our beloved 657.

You can post your notices--
yes, post all of them!--
and promise the journey is just the same,
with a few little changes to the route,
but we know it could never stand up to
our beloved 657.

Even the emails cannot move us,
although we invite you to continue sending them,
if only to save the trees from your notices;
still, your hawk-eyes at the drop-off point
will never stop us getting on
our beloved 657.

Great Misadventure (663)

It is not our bus.
It is another;
it is different.

Mark how the colour,
white, is not our colour,
red.

See the driver--
see how his face
is not Eric's.

Even the large,
orange numbers
are different.

Why, then,
do you remain
on the wrong bus?

'To have a great
misadventure, of course--
that is all.'

Comfort At Cost (641)

Money is not the only valuable asset
we have--in fact, we, as college students,
have very little of it at all,
but we have time.

I take my time from my pocket--
a little screwed up, a little damp--
and exchange it for a ticket
on the hourly 641.

Yes, there is the 640; it is fast
(one might call it 'dangerous'),
but my time is enough
for a little comfort.

Drifting through a hospital,
waiting by a sign for Lancashire,
wondering where on Earth I am--
but at least my seat is nice enough.

Section II - By Train

Police Investigation (WGN-BYN)

Always an excuse--
always someone to blame--
always another announcement--
always more minutes away.

Someone is running late--
someone is causing a fuss--
someone is past the yellow line--
someone is far too drunk.

One day it'll be here--
one day it won't run late--
one day the sun will shine--
one day we'll all be okay.

Pepper (RCD-SMB)

My love smells like lavender
in rolling, dew-damp fields
with buttercup petals drifting
from their fingers to their heels.

My home smells like familiarity
and dogs diving into rivers
with a tickle of endless paper
and the lingering scent of pizza.

For some reason, Smithy Bridge
smells like pepper--my literary
investigation of why, as ever,
continues.

Anything For You (BYN-DAR)

I know it has already been said
by others, about others,
that distance is no hindrance
to love of the purest kind,
but I feel the urge to remind you
that my affection is unwavering--
and yet, more than that:
my affection gives me strength
to destroy miles for you,
and the courage to make journeys
I would never have dreamed of making
on my own, not before--
but when you are the destination,
anything is possible--anything for you.

Disruption (WGN-MAN)

There are moments, small but potent,
when I, shaking, realise
that I am not everything.

I am not invincible, and a blade
would cut through me just like it would
through any other person.

These moments occur at the worst of times,
obviously, in dark alleyways
or unlit rooms, and I *do* shake.

Yet I continue. As of yet, no blade
has cut me down--no shadow
has snatched me,

and I know I'm running on luck and hope,
but I have a heart in my chest,
and it's still beating, so I walk.

Last Stepping Stone (RCD-LTL)

There is something to be said
about the last major station
that you hit
before arriving home.

There is relief
and a bittersweet acknowledgement
that your adventure is nearly over,
and the magic is fading.

Yet also, there is the allure
of familiar sights over new,
as you wave hello
to cows you knew as calves.

You can smile at signs
which have eroded under your eyes
after year, upon year,
upon long, long year.

Financial Insanity (BYN-WGN)

When coins equally line up to miles,
the sheep will neigh in glee.

I can guarantee that you'll never see
a happier rainbow bee.

You might as well take a moment
to observe the sky turning pink.

It already does that? Well, I think
the new polka dots are neat.

Make sure to check your train ticket
before your jaw bruises your feet.

At My Side (BYN-LDS)

A long journey never fails to feel shorter
with a friend by your side,
and if their adorable dog is by your feet--
well, the time just flies.

Gratitude feels too formal a word,
but thanks just don't feel right--
something in between lies in my heart
and forever will remain.

I do not think of it in every moment,
nor every waking hour of the day--
but whenever I do remember,
it brings a smile to my face.

Out Of Place (WGW-MCO)

Do you ever distinctly feel
like you do not belong in a room--
in fact, even further: that the room
was indeed intended for you,
yet has now been filled with others
who do not do what you do?

They do not worry, in youth, for money,
nor for distance, nor for work--
they travel by taxi, or they are dropped off,
and their smooth tongues
have been dipped in honey
from the early days of their birth.

No, I don't resent them, nor imply
they have no woes, but I do feel
out-of-place here--yet still,
like I *should* feel right at home.

Hopelessly Hopeless (LIV-SNH)

Yes, there are tears in my eyes
and a dead phone in my pocket
and the wrong ticket in my hand,
and I believe my voice did falter
and it was in the dead of night
and I did feel there was no hope
and no friends to fall back on
and not a chance in the world.

But I was wrong--and, for once,
to be wrong was the most beautiful
state in the world.

What I Know Now (OMS-LTL)

You cannot fully take the cold
from my shivering, creaking bones,
and though you may dry my eyes,
you cannot quell *all* the anxieties inside.

But that's alright,
because neither can I.

The warmth you give--
the eyes you dry--
the way you soothe my anxieties--
that is more than enough.

It always is,
and it always was.

Reverse Psychology (DAR-BYN)

Cheyenne is her name
and she is in my ear--
or rather, her lover is in my ear,
and he is speaking to her,
through me, and I only hope to meet her
so I may pass on his sweet thoughts.

Once, the want for you to want me
haunted me, accidentally,
but I have learned--I have evolved,
and now, a more experienced man,
I use my brain against itself:
you are my Cheyenne.

The Way Back (BYN-KEN)

Here, I left my life,
or parts of it, or all of it,
or none of it at all--
my memory is fuzzy,
but each field--each house--
they join the dots, bringing history
into focus, like the frames
caught in a scratched CD,
forever suspended, yet aided
by the mind's treasured images.

Habit-Forming (BYN-LTL)

I forget. How many times is it
to form a habit? How regular
must it be to be more
than coincidence, or hope
for habit?

If I say 'habit' one more time,
will it happen?

Nevermind. This is my own habit,
with my own rules,
and I say that it can exist--
I say that habit
is no more than this.

A returning journey,
for a returning kiss.

Worst Case Scenario (SNH-OMS)

You are a concept which lurks
in my nightmares, and I hate you
for existing--for threatening me,

constantly, with your utility--
and yet, your expense! God, no,
I cannot even consider you,

(think of my poor bank account,
weeping, and leave my thoughts!)
but you remain an option, nevertheless.

Into Your Heart (AUG-LIV)

Comfort and warmth linger
where you are--and now,
you allow me to be there,
too, accompanying you,
and my heart is glad.

This place is yours--
this situation, this journey--
and I am honoured
to be a part of it--
to be accepted.

If my eyes flutter closed,
just know I feel safe
with you beside me--
safe enough to let down my guard,
as I hope you will, too.

Expression (WGW-MCV)

Sometimes, you must look stupid
to be true--you must laugh
in an awkward way to be at ease--
you must open yourself,

revealing all the cracks
of your inner workings,

to find those who are broken,
and beautiful, and mended,
like you.

A Fortunate Miss (OMS-BYN)

Panic. Breathe. No. Release.

45

Danger. Dishonour. Screams. Silence.

Phone. Tears. Proposal. Accept.

Walk. Thanks. Cold. Cigarette.

House. Home. Blankets. Bed.

Riding On Euphoria (LDS-BYN)

Years. Three hundred and sixty five days,
over and over and over again.

Each second has been agony;
each day a heavier weight.

Waiting to wait to wait, again--
frustration painted with disappointment's brush.

Yet hope is alive. Hope is today.
Hope is this appointment, finally.

Our Ways Split (MCO-BYN)

The paths of our lives do not
run parallel--it is presumptuous
to say they run at all, as I do not,
personally, but the word remains on the page.

Sometimes, we are close enough to touch--
and we do.

We may dip away, from time to time,
and that is fine--I cannot always
hold your hand in mine.

Though I try.

But when we part, I always know
that at the end of both our roads
is a cosy junction where we can be
with each other, happily.

Between Sleep And Wake (LIV-AUG)

This train has become a sheep--
did you notice that? A very large,
spacious sheep, with comfortable seats,
and windows, and bathrooms...
oh, wait--this is still a train.

But look! The world outside
has become particles, colliding
into each other, forming shapes,
colours, people, almost like...
ah, just the normal outside world.

Then I suppose this daydream of a day,
when we have laughed, and hugged,
and known the comfort of closeness,
and now rest with eyes half-closed, half-open...
yes, this is true, too.

Section III - By Foot

Misty Morning Ache (WN4-WA11)

One foot. Two feet. Three feet.

Wait. Count again. One foot,
two feet, one foot--yes.

I am truly awake, even if
the street lamps still blaze,
giving glow to morning haze.

One foot. Two feet. Three feet.

Christ. Not again.

Regret, Unearned (WN5)

Allow me this--I beg,
one opportunity that is mine,
and mine alone--
my only request,
even if it sores my feet.

You can have your time,
and I can have mine,
and we can have ours.

Unlike everything else, time
is something we share enough of--
don't guard the tap
with your tongue
until it runs dry.

We can both cup our hands,
together and in turns,
for a while.

Aspects Of Childhood (OL15)

I suppose these little cards--
these 'fun facts', these cartoons
of smiling cats, jaguars--
are intended for younger ones,
like that little fairy house
and the imposing owl and mouse,
all carved from wood, once trees,
I suppose...

This is not for me,
and I know that,
but my enjoyment lasts.

Not For You (WN4-WN1)

Some journeys find themselves
with select participants,
chosen sporadically by fate
and assigned by destiny.

You may sigh at this,
but the truth does not change--
and know this: that journey
was only one of many.

Yes, friendship strengthened,
but only as it does on other days;
my enjoyment was not dependent
on the company, nor the route.

Pure Stubbornness (WN2-WN4)

We are young, we are free
and we make choices just because,
as we walk because we can
and we sing because we want
the entire world to know our joy,
or our sorrow, or our favourite
swear words.

Even if our way home
makes no sense to adult minds;
even if the knowledge
would drive our parents around the bend--
still, we will walk
and we will sing
and we will laugh.

To us, it isn't about the path--
we don't know what it *is* about,
but never that.

A Ruined Haven (L39-L40)

We have stumbled across
a wonderland--
it is silent
and it is beautiful.

They seek to take it from us,
gathering at the top of the rocks.

We know we cannot stop them,
and we know we won't try.

But for now--for these few,
faltering seconds--
this haven is ours.

Frozen Feet (LA9)

This is the long and lonely march,
where we, wearing our red blazers
with pride which would exist,
if we weren't so cold,
shuffle our feet and stamp the numbness
as if stamping will shake the lack of feeling.

It does not,
but we walk on,
because the bus has broken,
and there won't be another one.

This is the hardship of our parents--
this is the tale we were warned of,
and now we have been removed from comfort
and transported back to pre-civilisation.

Winter streets will not stop us,
and morning will not turn to noon
before we arrive at our destination
with frozen feet--or feet to be frozen,
soon.

Observed (WN5-WN4)

Two foxes have been following us,
diving into every long-running bush
to continue their sneaky observation.

Where do we walk? And why,
why do we walk?

Such questions plague foxes,
but not us--humans have no time
for this type of thought.

What are we saying? And when,
when will we stop?

Our chatter is not kind
to sensitive fox ears, but soon
we will cross a road, and promptly disappear.

Caretaker (WN1)

No, this child has never before
belonged to me. It could be said
that I've never had a child before,
and that would be correct.

Astoundingly correct, in fact;
one might call it a perfect answer.

Yet now there is a duty of care,
not legal but moral, put upon me,
by myself, and the ensuing journey
seems more an obligation than anything else.

Not a cruel, demanding obligation,
no, but an obligation, yes.

It will end, and the child will go,
and no ropes will attach me to them--
but my heart will be lighter,
and I will no longer be their caretaker.

Home After Midnight (WN2)

Rain becomes everything.
Once it begins, it consumes
and dampens, and drenches,
and turns dark into darkness;
this is our scene.

Midnight has a certain haunting,
eerie sense to it, like anything past
the deadest hour must be deader still,
including those walking through it;
this is our time.

Friendship, though--friendship
perseveres through conditions
which life would quake at,
laughing at despair with ease;
this is our reason.

Tracing Memory Lines (WN4)

A little girl took this route, once,
with a similarly little friend
and, sometimes, a little dog.

There is a man here, now,
wondering how everything
could have changed so much,

and yet not changed at all--
there is the park, the church,
and even the trees.

It seems like some things
haven't grown, while others
have blossomed beyond recognition.

Worry (M60-M3)

Maybe, if my fingers
curl around the little moon--
amethyst, if you're interested
in that sort of thing--
in my pocket a little tighter,
everything will be okay.

This is a falsehood,
plain and true,
but it comforts me.

In fact, it is a double falsehood,
as the reality is that nothing
will happen to me--of course,
this knowledge is from the future
and I am currently in the past.

Nevermind. This worry
won't last.

As A Ghost (WN4)

Sitting on damp grass
beneath the twilight shadow
of a great tree, I know
that no one would know
if anything were to happen to me.

This is how I imagine
a ghost would think,
but now a morbid tingling
is ruining my senses,
and I cannot hear.

Perhaps there is a ghost
beside me, wondering why
I am sitting, still and quiet,
pretending, perhaps, to be
dead, just like them.

To reassure the ghost,
I take in a breath, and watch
the misty cloud leave my lungs,
entering the chilled winter air,
never to be seen again.

Exhaust Me (OL15)

Every droplet of sweat,
if you'll forgive my crudeness,
is singing, or maybe screaming,
but I cannot stall myself now
so we must go on together.

Still, not all is awful here,
as the droplets cascade in shy cheer
to notice a sheep--a horse--a deer,
all watching our shared descent,
as we must go on together.

Down, down, then further down,
and every step is beauty, now,
with one hand shared in another's grasp
and the other is you, and I am tired,
but we must go on together.

Taken For Granted (WN4)

You were always an afterthought--
an option we had, but never chose
because our feet were enough
and the bus, even with a pass
which let us on for free, felt
like cheating, somehow.

Cheating on life,
I suppose.

Now, we can't even consider you,
because the cost outweighs the convenience,
yet you still exist,
don't you?

The bus' headlights are saddened eyes,
wondering why we never put out our hands
to signal it down, and take a seat.

Among The Roses (DL1)

Even one flower,
with delicate petals
and swirling colour
would be enough,
for me.

Yet you have found
an oasis of beauty,
and we have walked
within its presence,
and felt peace.

There is time after now,
and there has been time,
before now, and not all
is perfect, but this--
this is okay.

Up And Down (DL8)

The only issue with a downhill journey
is when you know you must return.

In some ways, an uphill beginning
is far more alluring.

At least then, you can look forward
to the ease of the way back.

But now there is a downhill slope;
later, there will be hardship.

A Short Commute (WN4)

Every day begins the same,
as marked by the to-do list
written in rainbow pen
and taped to the wall.

Every walk begins the same,
at the same time, down to
the very minute of leaving,
just to be consistent--

and it is only for consistency's sake,
because the commute pauses
at a house where time is in flux,
meaning the start of the journey

has no bearing on the end--
perhaps there is a random beauty
in that.

Migration (WN4-WN2)

Never before have I considered
our group of friends like this--
a herd, a charge, a force
to be reckoned with,
and when we move,
isn't it incredible
that we go meticulously
from house to house,
home to home,
seeking shelter or companionship
for or from
one of us;
one of ours.

Momentary Encounter (OL15)

See it--see it there,
but don't breathe,
don't speak--it might
leave, it might flee
if we make a move;
keep your arm close,
around me, and see.

From our vantage point,
on a fallen log within
a crowd of vertical logs,
we have the honour
of witnessing the deer
bending down to graze,
and isn't it beautiful?

No--no! Here comes
a hurtling bolt of red,
a dog--a dog! And our
friend, our charm,
our split-second wonder...
it is gone, and we are left
to pet the pet, and sigh.

Afterword

Even while I had other book ideas burning in my mind, or patiently waiting their turn, Commute jumped out and demanded my attention. I can't quite describe how that works, because that would require some sort of dissection of my mind which would be... difficult, to say the least, but it has led to the creation of this beautiful poetry collection.

From the cover to the poems themselves, I couldn't be prouder of this book. It encapsulates the multitude of emotions that I have felt while travelling, which has been a state that I have visited regularly - especially in my teenage years. These three sections are all slices of my life, prepared into neat poem formats for you to enjoy.

In the coming months, you can expect to see another poetry collection from me - On Gentle Wings - as well as the finale to my Cats Collection, Cats Home, which I am very excited to publish. But for now, I hope these words which cover the magic of movement have allowed you to fall in love with your commute - or at least enjoy it a little more!

As ever, stay safe and keep reading!

-Oskar Leonard.

Covers created with Canva. Some inner elements created
with Canva.

www.ingramcontent.com/pod-product-compliance
Lightning Source LLC
Chambersburg PA
CBHW052206150726

48002CB00003B/1137